TWO-HOUR NOSEW DECORATING

TWO-HOUR
NOSEW
DECORATING

DIANA
DUNKLEY

Sterling Publishing Co., Inc. New York
A Sterling/Chapelle Book

CHAPELLE LTD.

Owner
Jo Packham

Editor
Karmen Quinney

Staff
Marie Barber, Ann Bear, Areta Bingham,
Kass Burchett, Rebecca Christensen,
Brenda Doncouse, Dana Durney,
Marilyn Goff, Holly Hollingsworth,
Susan Jorgensen, Barbara Milburn,
Linda Orton, Leslie Ridenour,
Cindy Stoeckl, Gina Swapp

Photographer
Kevin Dilley/ Hazen Photography Studio
Page 79 Photo by Brianna Johnson

Library of Congress Cataloging-in-Publication Data

10 9 8 7 6 5 4 3 2 1

Published by Sterling Publishing Company, Inc.,
387 Park Avenue South, New York, NY 10016
© 2000 by Chapelle Limited
Distributed in Canada by Sterling Publishing
℅ Canadian Manda Group, One Atlantic Avenue, Suite 105
Toronto, Ontario, Canada M6K 3E7
Distributed in Great Britain and Europe by Cassell PLC
Wellington House, 125 Strand, London WC2R 0BB, England
Distributed in Australia by Capricorn Link (Australia) Pty Ltd.
P.O. Box 6651, Baulkham Hills, Business Centre, NSW 2153,
Australia
Printed in China
All Rights Reserved

Sterling ISBN 0-8069-9978-0

If you have any questions or comments, please contact: Chapelle Ltd., Inc., P. O. Box 9252 Ogden, UT 84409 (801) 621-2777 • FAX (801) 621-2788 • E-mail Chapelle1@ aol.com

ABOUT THE AUTHOR

Diana Dunkley

I was raised in Seattle, Washington, with seven sisters and a sewing genius for a mother. My home was filled with boxes and shelves of fabrics, laces, trims, batting, quilt squares, pins, needles, buttons, ribbons, and whatnot. Between mother and her eight girls there was always a sewing project going on. Most nights, we had to clear the kitchen table of patterns, fabrics, pins, and scissors before dinner could be served.

By the time I entered third grade, I was wearing a skirt that I'd made. In high school, I skipped the first year of sewing classes after bringing the teacher an arm load of clothes that I'd made. I then proceeded to take every sewing class offered, concluding with tailoring.

When I entered Brigham Young University, I jumped into the theatre arena. Here my appreciation of the art of sewing increased as I was immersed into the magical world of costume design. I loved the construction, rich fabrics, textures, trims, and enchantment created by the hands of the costume mistress. Last Christmas when I played the part of Glinda, the Good Witch in the Wizard of Oz, in Park City, Utah, I wasn't certain if I enjoyed my part or the costume more. (The glittered dress had a skirt with 26 layers.)

Creating this book has opened another avenue of expression and experimentation for me, the new world of NoSew decorating. I found that you don't have to be a seamstress to use fabric and it doesn't have to be difficult. As my daughter Abby said after making a NoSew shower curtain, "You can do almost anything NoSew if you just put your mind to it."

A Special Thanks to Abby Dunkley Krum, Michaeline Grassli, and Chapelle—especially, Jo.

DEDICATION

I dedicate this book to sewers in hopes that you will start thinking in a new unconventional way. I also give this book to nonsewers in hopes that you will begin a love affair with fabric, joining the ranks of sewers, filling your basements with boxes and shelves of fabric, trim, buttons, ribbons, batting, pins, scissors, and whatnot. Beware! It's never ending!

TABLE OF CONTENTS

INTRODUCTION

The day before Thanksgiving while I was in college, my friend and I jumped into his VW rabbit and drove all night to Seattle so that we could be home for Thanksgiving. Our trip was short. We had to be back in class Monday, so Sunday we started the long journey back to our apartments. What was it that compelled us to be so unreasonable—to drive all night? Of course, it was to be with family and friends on Thanksgiving; but it was especially mother with her beautiful Thanksgiving table and delicious food. My mother had created a refuge for me and my sisters. It was welcoming and clean, with bright colors and cheerful designs. My mother had created a home for all of us.

As years go by, I still get excited when I go home, and I have tried to identify what it is so that I can have it in my home, too. I have discovered along with love and tradition, your home's environment is very important. As you create a place of beauty and comfort, you will surround your family and friends with a feeling of worth, peace, and welcome.

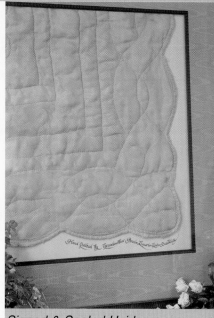

Signed & Sealed Heirloom

HOW CAN I MAKE THIS MINE?

One day after coming home from vacation, I realized how boring my home was. It was void of personal statement. I had wonderful antique pieces and great furniture, but they were things that could comfortably fit in any house. I was being careful and the result was no personal flair. That became the start of a new phase. I became outrageous in my attempt to break out of my comfort zone. At this point, decorating my home took on a passion and my tastes took on value. I began looking at everything with the question, "How can I make this mine?" That question opened a whole new way of looking at home decorating. For me, the best way to answer that question is to use fabric. Fabric adds color, texture, and design that is so needed, with limitless styles from which to choose. Upholstery stores offer richly colored fabrics with great texture. Discount outlets and the sale bins in the fabric stores offer a variety of fabric and trims.

Fabric used to be synonymous with sewing. This book will show you a new way. As you continue through the pages, you will find fabulous ways to use fabrics in your home and learn how to put them together in quick, easy ways without a sewing machine. You will find unusual ways to use place mats, napkins, scarves, and heirloom pieces. Look for the projects that appeal to you, then choose the colors and textures that will make them uniquely yours. Use the following pages as a springboard to create your own home decorating ideas.

Trust your instincts and ask yourself, "How can I make this mine?" Ideas will begin popping up everywhere. You will see items in a shop or in a book and you'll think, "that would be fabulous if I added . . ." or "I could make that myself" or "that gives me a great idea for this." This is called creativity. Give it rein and welcome aboard. As you generously contribute to the beauty of your home, you will be building a place of welcome for all who live and visit there and sending the silent message "come back soon."

STYLE

The most important aspect of home decorating is to develop your own style. Below are some tips on how to accomplish this.

- Be an observer.
- Start to recognize how you react to certain colors, textures, and styles.
- Keep a notebook of ideas that you love.
- Look through books, magazines, and catalogs. Cut out or copy anything that appeals to you. Jot down quotes, poems, or excerpts from literature that inspire you.
- Be attuned to colors, textures, and styles that give you pleasure or arouse passion in you.
- Surround yourself with items that will bring comfort and peace to your environment.
- Learn to trust your instincts.

Please Be Seated

COLORS & TEXTURES

Homes that call to us take time and consideration. Below are some tips on finding the right colors and textures that will work well with your personal and family's personality.

- Be an observer.
- Always be on the lookout for fabrics and objects that you find appealing.
- Place swatches of the colors and textures in the room where you think they will be used.
- Ask your family how they feel about colors and textures. *Beware of small swatches of fabric or paint. They are not large enough to give you a real sense for how they will read in a room.*
- When considering new fabrics, buy one yard or more of each fabric so that you can get a feeling of what the room will be like with that fabric.

SUPPLIES

FUSIBLE WEBBING

Fusible webbing is used to stiffen loosely woven fabrics and knits, to prevent dark background from showing through a light foreground, or to make frayable fabrics more manageable. It creates a crisp look. Different weights are made for different types of fabric. Fusible webbing comes in yards, ¼"-, and ½"-wide strips. Fusible webbing should be tested on sample fabric before using. If fusible webbing shows through fabric, cover with co-ordinating lace or trim.

GLUING

Fabric glue has a strong bond, dries quickly, and is transparent on most fabrics. Fabric glue should be tested on sample fabric before using. Make certain to keep glue lines clean and neat. Since fabric glues are not equal, try experimenting with different fabric glues to find one that best suits the fabric being used. Remember quality and strength of glue is important.

Some general supplies that might be helpful in creating the projects in this book: fabric weights for holding fabric in place; a measuring tape for measuring; button attaching kit for attaching buttons; a large clear plastic ruler for marking and drawing lines; ballpoint bodkin for ribbon weaving; and a small clear plastic ruler for measuring and marking hems, button placements, etc.

FABRIC SWATCHES

The projects in this book have been created using similar color palettes. Fabric swatches representing different color palettes and textures have been provided for your reference and to inspire your imagination. The various fabric swatches show the endless possibilities of color. The first step in planning any project, no matter how large or small, is to analyze the room in which the project will be placed. Colors can make a room look warm, cool, or relaxing. When different fabric types are used, the various textures add interest and variety to the decor.

These two pillows, at the left and below, were made using the same types of materials and same basic steps. To make these pillows, see Wrap & Tie Pillow on pages 64–65. A napkin ring adorns the knots on the pillow in the photograph to the left. Charms, beads, or ribbons could also be used. Experiment with different knots to create the desired look. The fabric on the pillow in the photograph below was simply twisted with ends tucked in.

Notice how the colors and textures of the fabrics on these two pillows, create a totally different mood for the same room. Remember, colors can stir our emotions and change our moods.

KALEIDOSCOPE CURTAINS

To make NoSew curtains, see Classic Curtains on pages 98–100. These curtains were made with panels of hand-painted fabrics and prestrung beaded trim. Two rods were used to hang the curtains. The sheer curtains were hung on the front rod and the heavier cotton or velvet curtains were hung on the second rod. This way any ambience or degree of light can be achieved. Pull the dark curtains, with the sheers accenting the ends and between sections for total darkness. Pull the sheers so the view is blocked but an abundance of light shows through, or both may be closed, creating an off and on dramatic effect.

VEILED CHAIR ELEGANCE

MATERIALS

Ready-made chair with cushion

Scarf

SUPPLIES

Staple gun and staples

INSTRUCTIONS

1. Remove cushion.

2. Stretch scarf with right side up over cushion. Staple to underside to secure.

3. Replace cushion.

MATERIALS

Neckroll pillow

Scarf: sized to cover neckroll pillow

Tassels on cording (2)

INSTRUCTIONS

1. Lay scarf with wrong side up on flat surface. Place neckroll vertically on scarf edge. Roll neckroll inward, wrapping neckroll in scarf.

2. Tie a tassel on each end.

BAUBLES & BEADS

INSTRUCTIONS

1. Cut piece of cardboard to size and shape of wire shelf top.

2. Lay fabric with wrong side up on flat surface. Place cardboard in center. Mark outline of cardboard. Remove cardboard. Cut fabric, adding 1" on all sides.

3. Lay fabric with wrong side up. Place cardboard on fabric. Wrap and adhere fabric to underside of cardboard, smoothing and trimming as necessary.

4. Place fabric-covered cardboard onto top of shelf.

5. String beads on beading wire as desired. Tie to secure.

6. Attach tassels as desired.

MATERIALS

Beading wire

Beads

Cardboard

Fabric

Tassels

Wire shelf

SUPPLIES

Craft scissors

Fabric glue

Fabric scissors

Shades of Cloth

Materials

Candlestand with glass shade

Fabric

Supplies

Fabric glue

Fabric scissors

This technique will work for lampshades as well.

Instructions

1. Remove glass shade from candlestand.

2. Adhere one fabric end to top of glass shade. Wrap fabric around glass shade slightly overlapping rows. Continue until entire glass shade is covered.

3. Trim excess fabric. Adhere fabric end to inside bottom edge of glass shade.

4. Place glass shade on candlestand.

PICTURE–PERFECT SETTING

MATERIALS

Fabric: double the size of picture frame

Foam-core board

Picture frame with glass

SUPPLIES

Craft knife

Fabric glue

Fabric scissors

Measuring tape

Spray adhesive

Stapler and staples

INSTRUCTIONS

1. Using craft knife, cut a piece of foam-core board to fit inside back of picture frame.

2. Using fabric scissors, cut fabric the same size as foam-core board. *Spray adhesive may change the color of fabric. Test before using.* Adhere fabric to foam-core board with spray adhesive, following manufacturer's instructions.

3. Place fabric side of foam-core board into frame.

4. Staple foam-core board to frame.

5. Using fabric scissors, cut a piece of fabric ⅛" larger on all sides than foam-core board. Adhere to back of frame.

RIBBON REMEMBRANCE

MATERIALS

Cording

Double photo mat board: sized to fit frame

Frame with glass

Mat board

Linen fabric

Trim: 3½"-wide; 1½"-wide

SUPPLIES

Fabric glue

Fabric scissors

Measuring tape

Spray adhesive

Be on the lookout for new and vintage pieces that can be framed. The trims used for this project consisted of embroidered grape leaves and imported velveteen.

INSTRUCTIONS

1. Cut fabric same size as mat board. Adhere fabric to mat board with spray adhesive, following manufacturer's instructions.

2. Cut trim and cording 2" shorter than length of mat board. *Measure carefully to make certain of even positioning on both sides.*

3. Arrange and adhere cording and trim onto fabric as desired. Allow to dry.

4. Place fabric and trim side of mat board down into photo mat board. Insert into frame and secure.

Shaped Coverlet

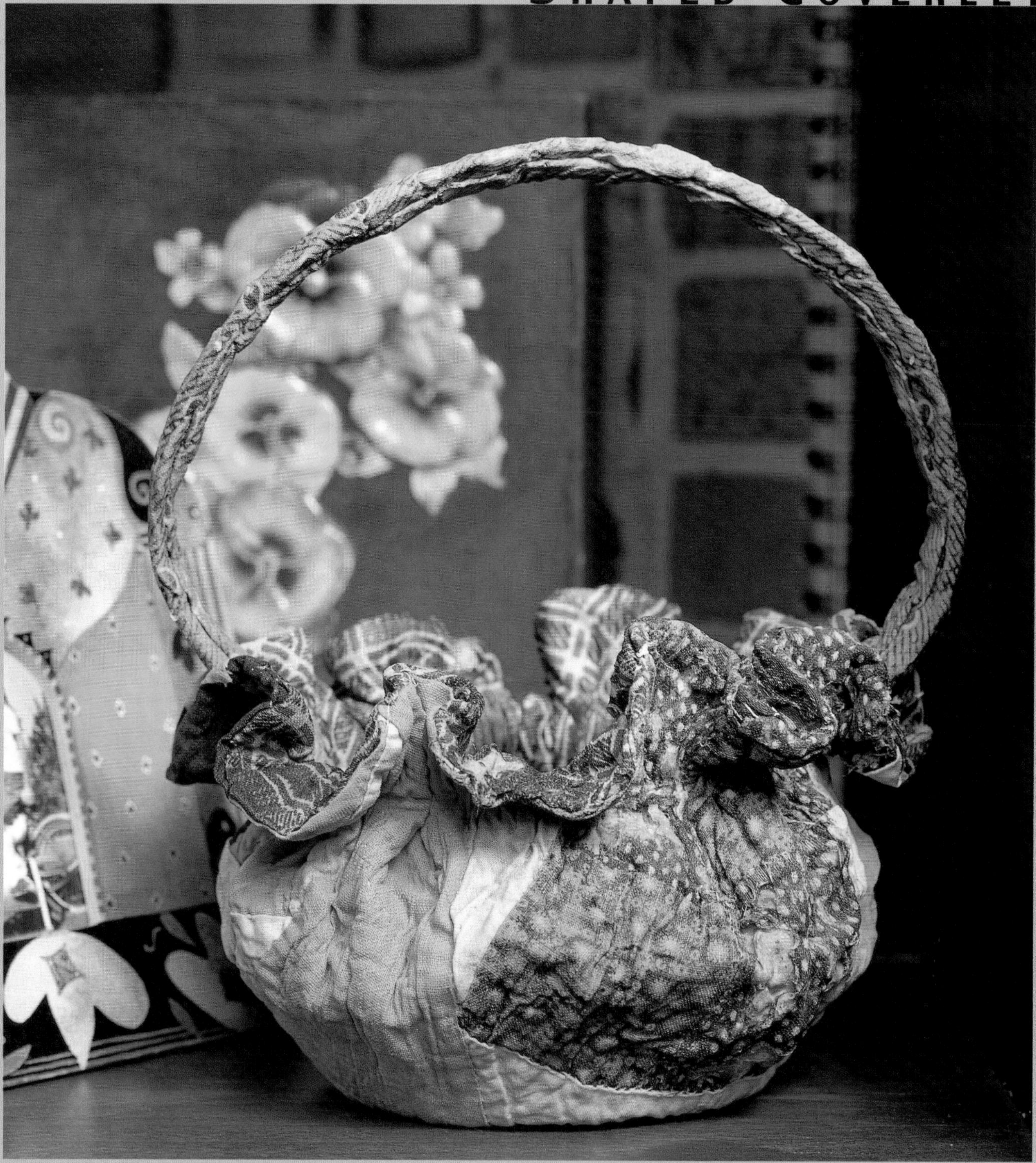

MATERIALS

Empty latex balloon

Old quilt piece

The look of the finished basket will depend on the shaping and molding process of the fabric while it is still wet.

SUPPLIES

Drinking glasses

Fabric glue

Fabric stiffener

Plastic wrap

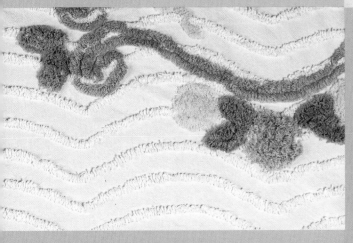

INSTRUCTIONS

1. Place plastic wrap over a flat surface, creating work surface.

2. Fill balloon with air to desired size.

3. Dip quilt piece into fabric stiffener, following manufacturer's instructions. Shape fabric around balloon as desired. Make certain to leave an opening.

4. Place project with open side down. Place drinking glasses upside down at even intervals around project. Shape fabric between and around drinking glasses, creating graceful ruffles for basket brim. Allow to dry.

5. Cut a strip from quilt piece as desired for handle. Dip strip into fabric stiffener. Shape handle to fit over bowl. Allow to dry.

6. Remove drinking glasses. Turn project right side up.

7. Adhere handle to basket.

8. Pop balloon and remove.

Acorn Adorned

Materials

Bugle beads

Fabric scraps

Papier-mâché egg

Seed beads

Twig

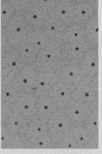

Supplies

Fabric glue

Fusible webbing

Glitter spray

Instructions

1. Place two fabric scraps of like fabric together. Apply fusible webbing to wrong side of one fabric scrap, following manufacturer's instructions. Fuse pieces with wrong sides together. *This stiffens fabric and prevents fraying.*

2. Cut desired petal shape from fused fabric scraps.

3. Run a thin line of glue along a few petal edges and dip edge into beads.

4. Pierce a small hole in top center of egg. Insert and adhere a twig, creating an acorn.

5. Adhere tip of petals to acorn top, layering and overlapping as desired.

6. Glitter-spray acorn.

Casual Cording

The choice of fabrics can make the same project look completely different.

Materials

Brass eyelets: ⅛" (16)

Cording: 2¼ yds.

Fabric: 1 yd.

Pillow form: 12"

Supplies

Eyelet pliers

Fabric glue

Fabric scissors

Instructions

1. Cut two 18" squares of fabric.

2. Fold hem in 1½" and miter corners. Adhere.

Mitering corners: Mark each corner to be mitered on a diagonal. See Diagram A.

Fold corner to back side. Cut off tip of folded corner. See Diagram B.

Fold one connecting side to back side. See Diagram C.

Fold remaining connecting side to back side. See Diagram D. Repeat for remaining corners.

3. Mark fabric square on right side two marks per corner 1" apart and two marks centered on each side 1" apart. Attach eyelets, following manufacturer's instructions. Repeat for remaining square.

4. Place pillow form between fabric pieces.

5. Cut 20" pieces of cording. Thread one piece through each set of eyelets and knot.

Heavy-weight fabrics work best for creating this pillow.

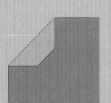

Diagram A

Diagram B

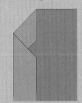

Diagram C

Diagram D

Snap
to
Perfection

Materials

Fabric: 54"-wide, 5⅓ yds.

Snaps (28)

Supplies

Fabric glue

Fabric marker

Fabric scissors

Measuring tape

Instructions

1. Cut fabric into two 94" sections.

2. Cut one section lengthwise into two sections. Make certain to match any repeat patterns before cutting.

3. Adhere ½" hem on all edges, except selvage edge.

4. Place uncut section onto a flat surface. Place remaining two panels on each side with selvage on outside edge.

5. Mark hemmed long edge of all side panels and selvage edge of uncut sections every 7".

6. Attach snaps on marks, following manufacturer's instructions.

7. Snap panels together.

Fabric yardage and quantity of snaps are for a double bed. Adjust dimensions as necessary.

MATERIALS

Door

Fabric: sized to fit door
  panels

SUPPLIES

Decoupage medium

Fabric scissors

Measuring tape

Sponge brush

Wallpaper spatula

When choosing a fabric, avoid border prints or stretchy fabrics.

INSTRUCTIONS

1. Cut fabric same measurement as door section to be covered. *Do not cut fabric too small. It is better to have excess fabric to trim down at door groove than not enough to cover the door.*

2. Apply decoupage medium to door.

3. Place fabric on door, stretching to edges. Using a wallpaper spatula and working from the center out, set fabric into place. Work out toward edges, covering entire area. Trim excess fabric at edges.

4. Apply decoupage medium over fabric. Using wallpaper spatula, work out any remaining air bubbles and/or wrinkles. Allow to dry.

5. Apply two additional coats of decoupage medium. Allow to dry between coats.

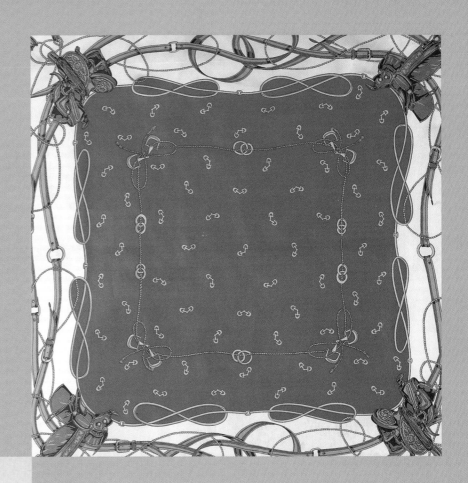

Silken Touch
Floor Cover

The type of canvas used for floorcloths is referred to commercially as "numbered duck canvas". This type of canvas will need to be primed with a coat of acrylic gesso before beginning. Priming prepares the surface by sealing the surface with moisture, producing a tight, dense backing. Or a preprimed canvas, referred to commercially as "floorcloth canvas", can be purchased ready to use. It is recommended that a rubber backing be placed onto the back side of the floorcloth. A rubber backing provides an element of safety, keeping the floorcloth from slipping when stepped upon. To clean floorcloth, wipe with damp cloth.

Instructions

1. Prime canvas with acrylic gesso if necessary, following manufacturer's instructions.

2. Using sponge brush, apply decoupage medium to entire canvas.

3. Center scarf right side up on canvas. Using hands, smooth scarf onto canvas, working out toward edges. Allow to dry.

4. Trim canvas even with scarf.

5. Cut four pieces of fabric to same length as scarf and 6" wide.

6. Run a thin line of glue ½" from edge on one side of scarf edge. See Diagram A.

7. Lay one piece of fabric wrong side up on scarf, matching edges. See Diagram B. Adhere. Allow to dry.

8. Fold fabric to back side, creating 3" binding. Adhere to back side. See Diagram C.

9. Repeat Steps 6–8 for remaining sides.

10. Adhere tassels to corners.

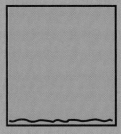

Diagram A

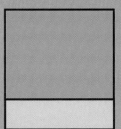

Diagram B

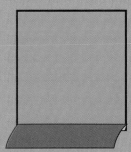

Diagram C

Materials

Fabric for canvas edging

Floorcloth canvas or numbered duck

Scarf

Tassels (4)

Supplies

Acrylic gesso (if using numbered duck)

Decoupage medium

Fabric glue

Fabric scissors

Measuring tape

Sponge brush

Materials

Curtain rod

Scarf

Instructions

1. Attach curtain rod brackets to wall, following manufacturer's instructions.

2. Place scarf on curtain rod. Arrange and pin corners to back side as desired. Remove scarf from curtain rod.

3. Adhere corners where marked with pins. Remove pins. Allow to dry.

4. Slide scarf onto curtain rod.

5. Place rod into brackets.

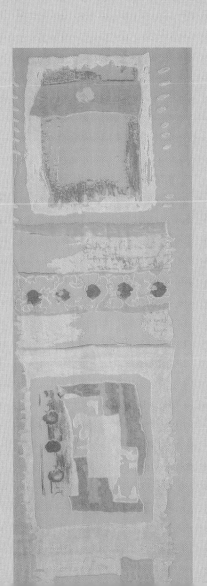

Supplies

Fabric glue

Straight pins

Gather in the Round

In place of displaying a tassel around the button, display beads or lace from a wedding dress, ribbons from a special bouquet of flowers, or metals or ribbons from a competition. Go beyond simply making a pillow, create a treasure.

MATERIALS

Buttons: 2" (2)

Coordinating cording: 60" (2)

Coordinating fabrics: 18" x 20" (2);
  20" x 36"

Round pillow form: 18"

Tassel

SUPPLIES

Fabric glue

Fabric marker

Fabric scissors

Fusible seam tape

Ironing board and iron

Measuring tape

Sewing needle

Thread

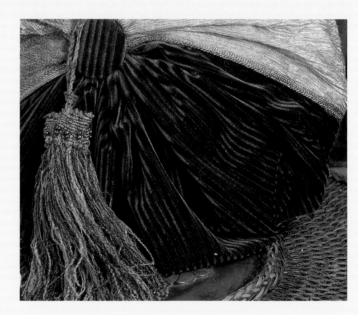

INSTRUCTIONS

1. Apply fusible seam tape to 20" right side edges of fabrics, following manufacturer's instructions. Fuse fabrics together, creating a tube. See Diagram A.

2. Cut each cording into three 20" lengths. Adhere one length of each along each seam on right side, making certain cordings are placed next to each other.

3. Find center on each side of pillow form and mark. Place pillow form inside tube. Place a running stitch around each end of tube. Pull thread on end of tube to gather fabric. See Diagram B.

4. Wrap a piece of thread around gathered material and knot thread. Trim ends of gathered fabric and thread. Repeat for other side.

5. Adhere one button in center of each side. *Buttons can be covered with a matching fabric, if desired.*

6. Wrap tassel around one button.

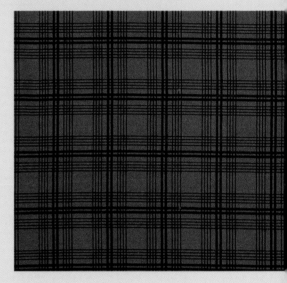

Diagram A

Diagram B

AUTUMN HARVEST

A 20" finished pumpkin would be considered a large pumpkin, 10" a medium finished pumpkin, and 6" a small finished pumpkin. Twice the fabric plus 4" of the desired diameter of finished pumpkin is needed. For example, a 44" circle makes a 20" finished pumpkin.

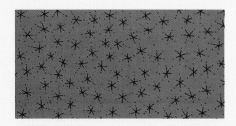

MATERIALS (for one pumpkin)

Fabric

Plastic pellets

Polyester stuffing

Ribbon

Stick for pumpkin stem

Wire

Wired grapevine

INSTRUCTIONS

1. Using fabric scissors, cut out circle as desired for pumpkin size.

2. Lay circle with wrong side up on a flat surface. Place two to three handfuls of plastic pellets in center of circle. Adjust as necessary for pumpkin size.

3. Place a mound of polyester stuffing on top of plastic pellets, covering two-thirds of circle.

4. Gather fabric by hand around polyester stuffing and hold tightly. *If a plumper pumpkin is desired, fill with more polyester stuffing and regather fabric.*

5. Wrap wire around gathered fabric. Pull wire tightly then twist to secure. Using wire cutters, cut wire.

6. Pull gathered ends of fabric up, making certain that all edges are up above wire.

7. Adhere stick inside opening, creating a stem.

8. Wrap wired grapevine around wrapped wire.

9. Remove a few leaves from grapevine and stuff into opening by stem and adhere.

10. Using fabric scissors, cut a piece of ribbon. Wrap ribbon around stem and leaves. Tie ribbon ends into a bow.

SUPPLIES

Fabric glue

Fabric scissors

Wire cutters

Keepsake
Pillow

When using a card that contains writing, make certain color copy is in reverse. Embellish pillow as desired.

Materials

Color copy of photo or card

Fabric: size of ready made pillow

Ready made pillow

Ribbon

Instructions

1. Apply photo transfer medium to color copy of photo or card. Place color copy wrong side up on middle of fabric. Transfer color copy to fabric, following manufacturer's instructions.

2. Adhere ribbon as desired for special contrast around picture. Adhere picture to pillow. *The photograph on this pillow was attached with matching ribbons.*

Supplies

Fabric glue

Photo transfer medium

Cover It Pretty

For a tablecloth that is tucked or puddles on the floor, add 1 yard to length. Table width must be width of desired fabric or smaller.

Instructions

1. Measure width and height of table. Add or subtract inches to height, depending on desired length and look. Cut fabric.

2. Center fabric on table, making certain it hangs equally on all sides.

3. Tuck and pin fabric around tabletop and legs as desired.

Materials

Bistro table

Fabric

Supplies

Measuring tape

Straight pins

INSTRUCTIONS

1. Cut fabric into ½"–¾"-wide strips.

2. Apply decoupage medium to starting point on chair and top edge of one fabric strip. *The chair leg bottom is a good starting point.*

3. Place top edge of fabric at an angle onto decoupaged section of chair. Begin wrapping chair, making certain to always overlap starting point. Next wrap should overlap previous wrap.

4. Repeat Steps 2–3, covering entire chair.

Paint desired parts of chairs before decoupaging and wrapping chair.

MATERIALS

Cotton fabric

Wrought iron chair

SUPPLIES

Decoupage medium

Fabric scissors

Measuring tape

Sponge brush

MATERIALS

Ready-made pillows

Sheer ribbon: 3"-wide, 20 yds.

SUPPLIES

Fabric glue

ROSETTE GARDEN

INSTRUCTIONS

1. Place pillows on bench. Wrap ribbon around each pillow, tying bows at front of bench.

2. Make and place rosettes as desired.

Making a rosette: Begin at one end and fold ribbon end forward at right angle. Fold vertical end of ribbon forward upon itself. See Diagram A.

Fold horizontal end of ribbon back and at right angle. Fold vertical ribbon over once. See Diagram B.

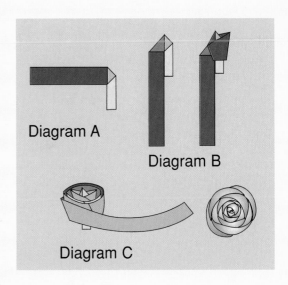

Diagram A

Diagram B

Diagram C

Continue folding ribbon, forming rosette. See Diagram C. Adhere bottom with glue.

Materials

D-ring

Fabric that holds a
crease

Wooden screen

Supplies

Fabric scissors

Fray preventative

Fusible seam tape

Ironing board and
iron

Measuring tape

Far East Corner

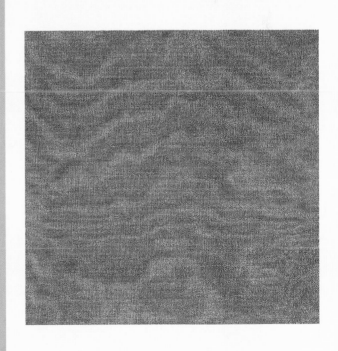

Instructions

1. Cut fabric slightly larger than screen opening.

2. Run a thin line of fray preventative along fabric edges, following manufacturer's instructions.

3. Place fabric on ironing board and D-ring on fabric as desired. Pull fabric up through ring and iron. Iron creases around ring. Allow to cool. Remove D-ring.

4. Repeat Step 3, covering entire fabric.

5. Fold top and bottom edges over 1" to make pocket. Apply fusible seam tape, following manufacturer's instructions. Fuse into place.

6. Slide rods from screen into top and bottom pockets and place rods in screen opening.

Shades of
Floral

Materials

Acrylic paints: metallic gold;
  off-white; coordinating color

Patterned fabric

Smooth fabric lampshade

Spray paint: off-white

Lightweight fabrics work best.

Supplies

Decoupage medium

Fabric scissors

Paintbrushes

Sea sponge

Sponge brushes (2)

Two-part crackle medium

Instructions

1. Spray-paint inside of lampshade. Allow to dry. Using sponge brush, paint outside of lampshade with metallic gold paint. Allow to dry.

2. Apply coat of part one crackle medium over gold paint. Allow to dry.

3. Using remaining sponge brush, paint over crackle medium with off-white acrylic paint. Allow to dry.

4. Apply coat of part two crackle medium. Allow to dry.

5. Using sea sponge, sponge top and bottom binding of lampshade with coordinating acrylic paint.

6. Cut out desired motifs from fabric, creating appliqués.

7. Arrange appliqués on lampshade as desired. Remove appliqués one at a time and apply decoupage medium to lampshade and secure appliqués in place. Allow to dry.

8. Apply decoupage medium over appliqués. Allow to dry.

CURTAIN CALL

To make NoSew curtains, see Classic Curtains on pages 98–100. Several inches have been added onto the length of these drapes so that they puddle on the floor. These drapes are adorned with beaded tassels. Also, there is a mixture of sheer and opaque fabrics so that you can spread out the sheer panels and let the light through. Or scrunch the sheer panels and spread out the opaque panels for more privacy. It's your call.

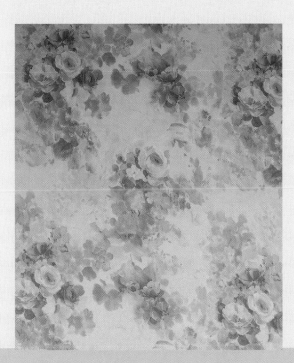

SHEER TABLE SARONG

The fabric yardage is for a standard decorative round table. For best results, place a base tablecloth on table before starting.

INSTRUCTIONS

1. Cut two 54" squares.

2. Place one square over table. Place next square so that ends hang down opposite of first square. Tuck corners under.

3. Wrap remaining fabric around top outside edge of table. Tie a knot. Start to tie another knot, but do not pull fabric through, leaving it in a loop. See photograph on facing page.

4. Pin loop in place.

MATERIALS

Sheer fabric: 6 yds.

SUPPLIES

Fabric scissors

Measuring tape

Safety pins

Materials

Ready-made pillow

Sheer fabric

Tassels on cording (3)

Wrap & Tie

Instructions

1. With wrong side of fabric facing up, place pillow face down diagonally on center of fabric. See Diagram A.

2. Bring two ends of fabric up and cross over. See Diagram B. Turn pillow over.

3. Cross over and tuck one end under fabric. See Diagram C.

4. Cross over and tuck remaining end under fabric. See Diagram D.

5. Tie a knot on top with fabric ends to secure. Tuck unfinished ends under.

6. Tie tassels around knot as desired.

A 16" pillow requires three yards of fabric. Adjust as necessary.

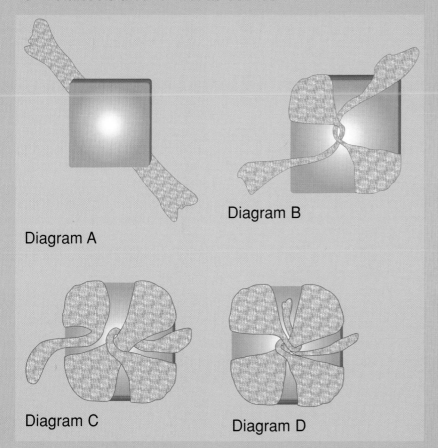

Diagram A

Diagram B

Diagram C

Diagram D

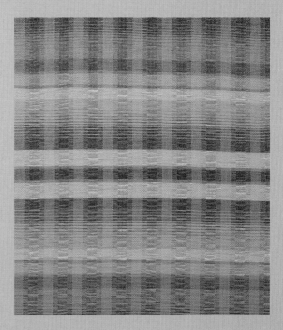

Hand Quilted by Grandmother Annie Laurie Lowe Dunkley

Frame with glass

Heirloom

Photo mat

Photo mat board

INSTRUCTIONS

1. Mount photo mat board to foam-core board. Arrange heirloom as desired on photo mat board. *Large items may be cut to a smaller size as desired.*

2. *Two edges of heirloom will be pinned down.* Starting in middle of one edge, pin heirloom to back side edge of foam-core board. Make certain to place pins equal distance apart. Repeat for connecting edge. *The glass on the frame will keep unpinned edges from shifting.*

3. Place photo mat on top. Insert photo mat into frame and secure.

For an extra special touch, add a name, date, or saying onto mat.

SUPPLIES

Stainless steel pins

SIGNED & SEALED HEIRLOOM

Here is an idea that can help display heirlooms. This quilt was falling apart, but we were able to cut out and save several good pieces of the quilt. These were framed and distributed to other family members. An embellished pillow as shown on the left can also be framed.

OLD-TIME COMFORT

MATERIALS

Batting

Fabric

Legs (4)

Pine: ¾"

Plywood: ½"

SUPPLIES

Color stain

Fabric scissors

Glue gun and glue sticks

Jigsaw

Measuring tape

Nails

Pencil

Staple gun and staples

Wood glue

Pilot holes should be drilled before nailing to avoid splitting wood.

12"

13½"

Diagram A

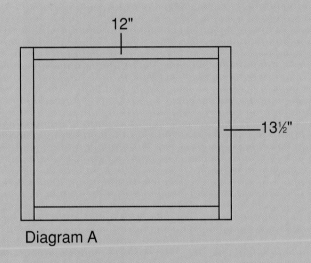

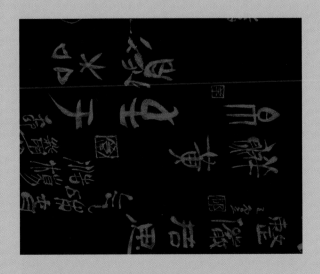

INSTRUCTIONS

1. Using jigsaw, cut two 2½" x 12", and two 2½" x 13½" pieces of pine.

2. Using jigsaw, cut two 14½" x 11½" pieces of plywood, creating top and bottom.

3. Stain all wood pieces except top and bottom pieces. Stain legs.

4. Using wood glue, adhere 12" pieces of wood to ends of 13½" pieces of wood, creating box. See Diagram A. *Three nails have been used per side for extra hold.*

5. Adhere bottom to box.

6. Cover top with 15½" x 12½" piece of batting. Using glue gun, adhere into place.

7. Using fabric scissors, cut 17" x 14" piece of fabric.

8. Place fabric with wrong side up on a flat surface. Center plywood with batting side facing down. Pull fabric taunt on each side, pleating corners and stapling excess fabric to back side.

9. Adhere top to box.

10. Adhere one leg to each bottom corner of box. Allow to dry.

MATERIALS

Fabric: 5½" x 35"

Ready-made pillow: 18"

Ribbon: 2 yds.

SUPPLIES

Fabric glue

Fusible seam tape

Measuring tape

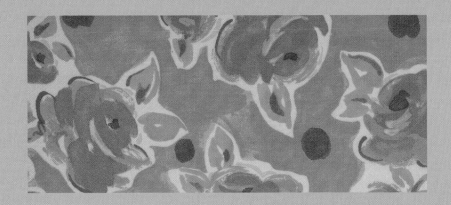

SIMPLY TIED

INSTRUCTIONS

1. Apply fusible seam tape to 35" sides of fabric, following manufacturer's instructions. Fuse hem to wrong side, finishing edges.

2. Apply fusible seam tape to one short end. Fuse ends of band, forming a circle.

3. Slip band around pillow and center. Band should be tight.

4. Wrap ribbon around band and tie ribbon ends into a bow.

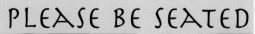

PLEASE BE SEATED

MATERIALS

Ribbon: 1½" yds.

Self-adhesive velcro

Upholstery fabric

SUPPLIES

Fabric glue

Fabric scissors

Measuring tape

INSTRUCTIONS

1. Measure width and depth of chair seat plus 10" for width and 5" for depth. See Diagram A.

2. Measure width of chair back plus 1¼". Measure height of chair back and double plus 1¼".

3. Cut out chair back and chair seat covers. Make certain any design in fabric is centered to coincide with chair seat.

4. Adhere ½" hem around edges.

5. Cut sixteen 18" lengths of ribbon.

6. Cut sixteen 1½" lengths of velcro.

7. Fold chair back fabric in half with right sides together.

8. Adhere loop side of velcro piece 4" down from fold on each wrong side of fabric. Adhere loop side of velcro piece ⅛" from bottom edge on each wrong side of fabric. Adhere loop side of velcro piece centered between the two on each side.

9. Adhere ribbon lengths to hook sides of velcro pieces. Attach velcro pieces together. Repeat for facing side. See Diagram A.

10. Adhere loop side of velcro pieces to chair seat cover. See Diagram B. Adhere hook side of velcro pieces to corresponding ribbon lengths. Attach velcro pieces together.

11. Place chair back and chair seat on chair and tie ribbons into a bow.

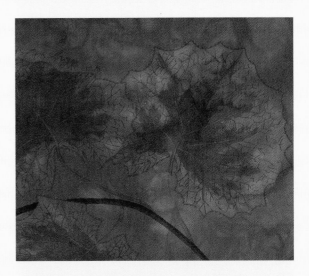

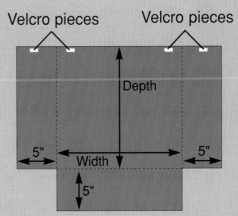

Diagram A

Diagram B

73

Materials

Fabric for edging

Fabric for throw

Supplies

Fabric glue

Fabric scissors

Ironing board and iron

Measuring tape

Warm Encounters

Instructions

1. Cut fabric to desired size for throw.

2. Place throw fabric with right side up on a flat surface.

3. Cut four pieces of coordinating fabric to length of throw plus ½" and 6½"-wide.

4. See Steps 6–8 of Silken Touch Floor Cover on page 39 for finishing throw.

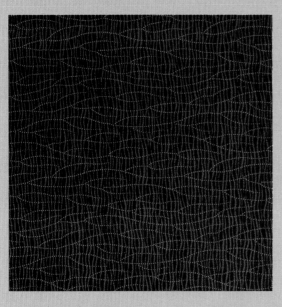

INSTRUCTIONS

1. Make certain fabric edges are straight.

2. Using paint roller, apply wall covering adhesive to wall, following manufacturer's instructions.

3. Using two people, lift short end of fabric to ceiling. Pull tightly across top edge and begin to straighten and smooth into place. Using wallpaper spatula, remove any air bubbles. *Make certain to keep adhesive off the face of the wallcovering as it may cause permanent discoloration. Excess adhesive should be removed immediately with a damp cloth.*

WALL WONDERMENT

Wall covering adhesive works best with lightweight fabrics. Make certain the surface is clean, dry, smooth, and structurally sound before beginning.

MATERIALS

Lightweight fabric: sized to fit from floorboards to ceiling

SUPPLIES

Paint roller

Person to help

Wall covering adhesive

Wallpaper spatula

RAINBOW
OF RIBBONS

My inspiration for the hanging ribbons came from my daughter Olivia's wedding veil. The traditional veil just did not fit Olivia's personality. Finally, we threw the tulle away and ventured into a totally new direction. Ribbons. Lots and lots of ribbons. We bought varying sizes, hues, and textures, and adhered them onto a clip. She wore the clip beneath layers of curls. The ribbons trailed behind her, draped over her shoulder, and billowed in the wind. The effect was enchanting. After the wedding, she hung them on the wall in her apartment.

MATERIALS

Brackets (2)

Decorative curtain rod

Seven coordinating ribbons: (8 yds. each)

SUPPLIES

Fabric scissors

Measuring tape

INSTRUCTIONS

1. Attach curtain rod brackets to wall, following manufacturer's instructions.

2. Cut one type of ribbon 3⅓ yds.

3. Fold ribbon in half. Place fold over rod, creating loop. See Diagram A.

4. Pull ribbon ends through loop. See Diagram B. Pull tightly.

5. Slide ribbon to left, forming longest ribbon.

6. Cut 1 yd. of second ribbon. Repeat Step 3. Slide ribbon to right, forming shortest ribbon.

7. Repeat Steps 3–4. Beginning at left, cut each additional ribbon slightly shorter until first and second ribbons meet.

8. Place curtain rod into brackets.

Diagram A

Diagram B

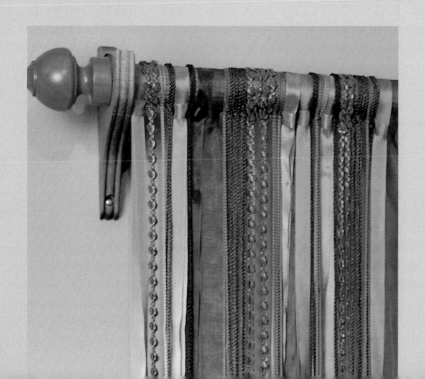

Materials

Fabric motifs

Foam-core board: sized to fit frame

Frame with glass

Photo mat

Supplies

Fabric glue

Fabric scissors

Finely Framed

When choosing fabric, remember that upholstery and drapery fabrics offer a wide variety of prints.

Instructions

1. Cut out desired motif to fit into photo mat.

2. Adhere motif to foam-core board.

3. Insert photo mat and foam-core board into frame and secure frame.

Lightweight, tightly woven fabrics work better than others for this project. Decoupage medium may change the color of some fabrics. Make certain to test fabric with decoupage medium before beginning. The lighter weight fabrics without a nap are more effective. (A sheer crinkle fabric was used for project pictured.) The size of floorcloth canvas will be limited to width of fabric.

The type of canvas used for floorcloths is referred to commercially as "numbered duck canvas". This type of canvas will need to be primed with a coat of acrylic gesso before beginning. Priming prepares the surface by sealing the surface with moisture, producing a tight, dense backing. Or a preprimed canvas, referred to commercially as "floorcloth canvas", can be purchased ready to use.

MATERIALS

Fabric

Floorcloth canvas or numbered duck canvas

SUPPLIES

Acrylic gesso (if using numbered duck)

Decoupage medium

Fabric scissors

Measuring tape

Sponge brush

FLOORCLOTH FANCY

INSTRUCTIONS

1. Prime canvas with acrylic gesso if necessary, following manufacturer's instructions.

2. Cut fabric 2" larger than canvas on all sides.

3. Using sponge brush, apply decoupage medium to entire canvas.

4. Center fabric right side up on decoupaged canvas, allowing 2" excess on all sides. Using hands, smooth fabric onto canvas, working out toward edges. Allow to dry.

5. Apply decoupage medium over fabric. Allow to dry.

6. Apply decoupage medium to wrong side of overlapping fabric. Fold excess fabric to back of canvas. Smooth and round out corners. Allow to dry.

7. Apply two additional coats of decoupage medium to front and back of canvas. Allow to dry between coats.

It is recommended that a rubber backing be placed onto the back side of the floorcloth. A rubber backing provides an element of safety, keeping the floorcloth from slipping when stepped upon. To clean floorcloth, wipe with damp cloth.

RIBBON WRAPPED

INSTRUCTIONS

1. Mark cloth napkins on right side in center of all four sides and 2" in from edge.

2. Attach eyelets on napkins sides as marked, following manufacturer's instructions.

3. Cut ribbon into four equal pieces.

4. Place napkins on either side of pillow, lining up eyelets.

5. Thread ribbon through eyelets and tie ribbon ends into a bow.

MATERIALS (for one pillow)

Eyelets: ¼" (8)

Hand-dyed silk ribbon: 2 yds.

Square cloth napkins: sized 4" larger than pillow (2)

Square pillow

SUPPLIES

Eyelet pliers

Fabric marker

Fabric scissors

Measuring tape

Materials

Prestrung beads

Scarf

Supplies

Fabric glue

Dressed Up & Beaded

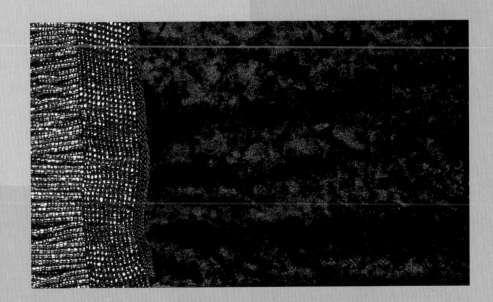

Instructions

1. Lay scarf right side up on flat surface.

2. Adhere prestrung beads to scarf edges as desired.

INSTRUCTIONS

1. Cut fabric to desired length and width. *If using width as length, the selvage edge will need to be trimmed in order to fringe.*

2. Unravel short ends of runner to desired length for fringe.

3. Fold ½" hem on long edges of runner. Apply a strip of fusible seam tape along hems, following manufacturer's instructions. Fuse into place.

4. Comb out fringe with fingers and separate into 1" sections .

5. Tie every other section together in a knot.

FRAZZLED & FRINGED

Medium- to heavy-weight fabrics work best.

MATERIALS

Fabric

SUPPLIES

Fabric scissors

Fusible seam tape

Ironing board and iron

Measuring tape

LIGHTLY COVERED

INSTRUCTIONS

1. Paint light switch plate screws. Allow to dry.

2. Place fabric with wrong side up on a flat surface.

3. Place light switch plate on fabric and trace outline. Remove light switch plate. Cut out shape, adding 1" on all sides.

4. Center light switch plate on wrong side of fabric and trace center opening. Cut an "X" in opening from corner to corner. Fold clipped fabric back through opening and adhere.

5. Pull fabric on sides to back side and adhere.

6. Cut ⅜" square from each corner, removing excess fabric. Fold remaining fabric at each outside corner to back side. Pull fabric tightly and adhere to light switch plate.

MATERIALS

Acrylic paint

Fabric

Light switch plate

SUPPLIES

Fabric glue

Fabric marker

Fabric scissors

Measuring tape

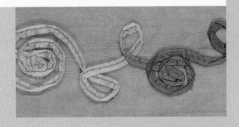

Candlestand with glass shade

Ribbon: 1⅜"-wide, 4 yds.

SUPPLIES

Fabric glue

Fabric scissors

INSTRUCTIONS

1. Remove glass shade from candlestand.

2. Fold ribbon under ¼" lengthwise. Adhere one ribbon end to top of glass shade. Wrap ribbon around glass shade, overlapping rows. Continue until entire glass shade is covered.

3. Trim excess ribbon. Adhere ribbon end to inside bottom edge of glass shade.

4. Place glass shade on candlestand.

SHADES OF RIBBONS

Floral Accents

Medium-weight fabrics with no distinct or geometric pattern work best. Different fabrics can be used for the top, bottom, and the wrap for the box.

Materials (for one box)

Coordinating cording

Eyelets: ⅛"

Fabric

Lace appliqués (2)

Papier-mâché box with lid

Supplies

Eyelet pliers

Fabric glue

Fabric marker

Fabric scissors

Measuring tape

Instructions

1. Measure box. Cut a square of fabric large enough to cover bottom and sides of box plus 2".

2. Lay fabric with wrong side up on a flat surface.

3. Place bottom of box in center of fabric, making certain box is square with fabric. Mark fabric on all sides of box, bringing lines to edges. See Diagram A on page 96.

4. Remove box. Cut out squares along dotted lines in each corner to ½" from marked lines, removing excess fabric. See Diagram B on page 96.

5. Place and adhere bottom of box onto center of fabric.

6. Clip fabric to ¼" at each corner of box.

7. Adhere fabric onto two opposite sides of box. Pull fabric tight, wrapping around sides and over top of box. See Diagram C on page 96.

8. Repeat with remaining two sides. Fold in excess side fabric and adhere to box.

9. Repeat Steps 1–8 for lid of box.

(continued on page 96.)

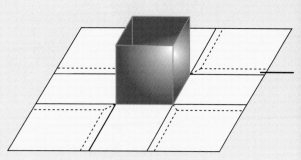

Diagram A

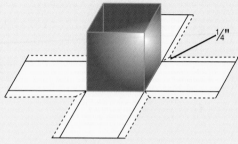

$\frac{1}{4}$"

Diagram B

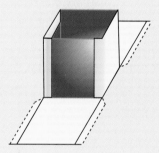

Diagram C

11. Fold and adhere ½" hem along length of cut fabric. Fold fabric in thirds, with right sides out, overlapping raw edge with hemmed edge. Adhere.

(Continued from page 95.)

Box Wrap

10. With lid on box, measure around box beginning at top, plus 6". Cut fabric to desired width.

12. Adhere cording around one short end. Trim remaining unfinished edge by adhering a lace appliqué onto right side.

13. Center two eyelets 1" from end of fabric and 1" apart. Attach eyelets on fabric, following manufacturer's instructions. Repeat on opposite end.

14. Place wrap around box and position lace appliqué on front of box.

15. Cut cording to desired length. Thread cording through all four eyelets and tie a bow. Adhere another lace appliqué onto top center of wrap.

Classic Curtains

When determining the length of the drapes, keep in mind the following questions: How high will the rod be? How long do you want the drapes? The width of fabric should be double the width of opening. A drapery table is wonderful if you have access to one. It contains all the measurements for precise cutting.

Materials

Coordinating fabric

Cording

Curtain rings (*Curtain rings should be placed every 4".*)

Curtain rod

Eyelets: ¼"

Ribbon: ¼"-wide

Supplies

Eyelet pliers

Fabric glue

Fabric scissors

Fusible seam tape

Ironing board and iron

Measuring tape

Instructions

(Photo on page 98.)

1. Cut panels of fabric according to desired measurements. Add 7½" for hems. *Be very precise with measurements since they determine how straight drapes will hang.*

2. Fold selvage edge in 1" to back side and apply fusible seam tape, following manufacturer's instructions. Fuse into place.

3. Press 2" hem on top of drape panel. Apply fusible seam tape and fuse into place.

4. Fold top hem over again and adhere.

5. Press 3½" hem on bottom and apply fusible seam tape along top edge of hem. Fuse into place.

6. Adhere ribbon over hem to keep it from fraying.

7. Mark top edge every 4" for eyelet placement. Attach eyelets on fabric, following manufacturer's instructions.

8. Cut 24" piece of cording for each eyelet. Thread cording through top of each eyelet.

9. Tie drapes to rings. Place rings on curtain rod.

Shades of Silk

This is a variation of Silken Panel on page 40. However, this curtain rod has been placed in a window and the scarves are attached by knotting them onto the curtain rod.

MATERIALS

Coordinating acrylic paints (2)

Fabric

Foam pad: 4" thick

Handle

Legs (4)

Old drawer

Plywood: double the size of drawer

Supplies

Fabric scissors

Glue gun and glue sticks

Paintbrushes

Saw

Screwdriver and screws

Sea sponge

Serrated kitchen knife

Staple gun and staples

Varnish

Wood glue

Instructions

1. Using saw, cut a piece of plywood to exact outside size of drawer. Cut another piece of plywood to fit inside drawer.

2. Using paintbrush, paint drawer and middle section of legs with one shade of acrylic paint.

3. Using paintbrush, paint top and bottom of legs with second shade of acrylic paint.

4. Using sea sponge, sponge drawer with second shade of acrylic paint.

5. Using wood glue, adhere legs to underside of drawer.

6. Varnish wood pieces, following manufacturer's instructions.

7. Screw on handle.

8. Using serrated kitchen knife, cut foam pad slightly larger than larger plywood piece. Using glue gun, adhere foam to larger plywood piece.

9. Place foam/wood piece foam side down onto wrong side of fabric. Cut fabric to fit wood piece, plus 5" on all sides. Pull fabric taut and staple to wood, easing in corners and pleating as necessary.

10. Using fabric scissors, cut off excess fabric.

11. Using wood glue, adhere smaller plywood piece to bottom of foam/wood piece, creating seat. Allow to dry.

12. Using wood glue, adhere seat to stool.

FLOWERS WITH A FLARE

When using floral fabrics, choose motifs with flowers and leaves that can be easily cut out. Choose one floral fabric that is neutral and subtle for the background fabric.

MATERIALS

Coordinating floral fabrics

Double photo mat

Foam-core board: sized to fit frame

Frame with glass

Thin cording

SUPPLIES

Fabric glue

Fabric marker

Fabric scissors

Fusible webbing

Ironing board and iron

Solid-head pins: ½"

INSTRUCTIONS

(Photo on page 104.)

1. Set background fabric aside. Cut out motifs from floral fabrics, creating appliqués. Apply fusible webbing to wrong side of appliqués, following manufacturer's instructions.

2. Lay background fabric with wrong side up on a flat surface. Place foam-core board in center. Mark outline of foam-core board. Remove foam-core board. Cut fabric, adding 2½" on all sides.

3. Lay fabric with right side up on a flat surface. Arrange appliqués on background fabric as desired. Fuse into place.

4. Loop and wind cording on fabric as desired. Adhere cording in place.

5. Lay fabric with wrong side up on a flat surface. Place foam-core board in center. Start in middle of each edge and push pins in edge of foam-core board. Make certain to place pins equal distance apart.

6. Insert photo mat into frame. Place fabric side of foam-core board into frame and secure.

Comforting Touch

Materials

Fleece fabric: 54"-wide, 1⅛ yds.

Ribbon: 8 yds.

Supplies

Fabric scissors

Measuring tape

Instructions

1. Round corners of fleece fabric.

2. Cut 2" slits in fabric edges, creating fringe.

3. Cut 18" pieces of ribbon.

4. Tie ribbon in a double knot around two pieces of fringe. Skip three pieces of fringe and tie another ribbon.

5. Repeat Step 4 until blanket fringe is complete.

SUN, SHADE, AND LACE

INSTRUCTIONS

1. Measure width and length of window shade plus 1" on all sides.

2. Cut lace to match above measurements.

3. Place window shade with right side up on a flat surface.

4. Place lace with right side up onto window shade. Neatly, fold excess lace to back and adhere. *Remember people will see the back of the window shade, so make it look nice.*

5. Adhere fringe at bottom.

MATERIALS

Fringe: enough to cover bottom width of window shade

Lace: enough to cover window shade

Window shade

SUPPLIES

Fabric glue

Measuring tape

LOVELY LACED COMFORT

MATERIALS

Cloth napkins with cutwork: 18" (2)

Cording: 4 yds.

Lace doily: sized to fit napkin

Pillow form: 14"

SUPPLIES

Ballpoint bodkin

Fabric glue

Fabric scissors

Fusible webbing

INSTRUCTIONS

1. Apply fusible webbing to wrong side of lace doily, following manufacturer's instructions.

2. Lay napkin with right side up on a flat surface. Arrange lace doily on napkin as desired. Fuse into place.

3. Place napkins with wrong sides together. Cut cording into four 1-yard lengths. Using one length per napkin side, lace cording through cutwork with ballpoint bodkin. Lace three sides together, leaving 12" of cording on each end for bows.

4. Insert pillow form into laced napkins.

5. Lace remaining side.

6. Tie a bow in each corner.

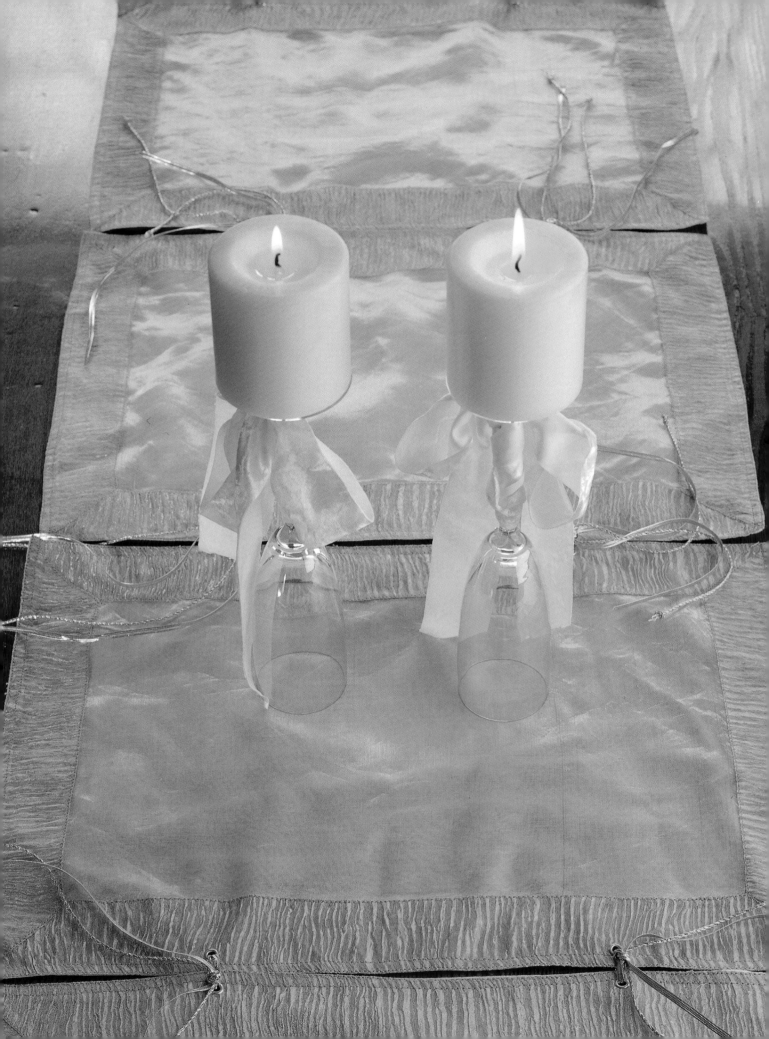

Contemporary Ties

Instructions

1. Lay placemats with right sides up, side by side. Mark 1" up from top and bottom edges and 5" in from side edges for eyelets. See Diagram A.

2. Attach eyelets on fabric, following manufacturer's instructions.

3. Cut eight 18" pieces of cording and trim.

4. Thread one piece of cording and one piece of trim through eyelet of one placemat into eyelet of the next. Knot.

5. Repeat until all placemats are joined.

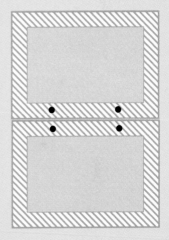

Diagram A

Materials

Cording: 4 yds.

Eyelets: ⅛" (16)

Placemats (5)

Trim: 4 yds.

Supplies

Eyelet pliers

Fabric glue

Fabric scissors

Measuring tape

113

TIMELESS TAPESTRY

MATERIALS

Coordinating cording

Coordinating tassels (3)

Decorative curtain rod: sized slightly
  larger than tapestry

Tapestry

SUPPLIES

Fabric glue

Straight pins

*If using an antique tapestry, do not
use glue. Glue will destroy its value.
Instead, baste or pin the tapestry
over the rod.*

INSTRUCTIONS

1. Attach cording to curtain rod,
creating a hanger.

2. Place tapestry on curtain rod.
Arrange and pin top to back side as
desired. Remove tapestry from
curtain rod.

3. Adhere top where marked with
pins. Remove pins. Allow to dry.

4. Slide tapestry onto curtain rod.

5. Tie tassels onto rod as desired.

Materials

Buttons (4)

Fabric: 30" x 29"

Pillow form: 12"

Supplies

Button attaching kit

Fabric scissors

Fusible seam tape

Iron and ironing board

Measuring tape

Instructions

1. Cut 30" x 29" piece of fabric.

2. With right sides together, apply fusible seam tape along 30" edges. Fuse together, creating a tube.

3. With wrong sides together, press a 4" hem at both ends. Apply fusible seam tape and fuse hem into place. Turn right side out.

4. Place pillow form into middle of tube. Adjust seam to be center back.

5. Place two buttons 2½" from pillow form and 3" from edges of fabric. See photograph. Attach buttons with button attaching kit, following manufacturer's instructions.

6. Repeat Step 5 on opposite end of pillow.

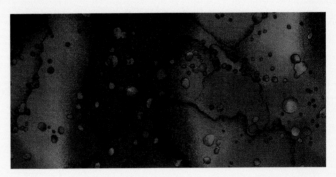

Fall Delight Curtains

Materials

Curtain rod: 1¼"

Lightweight fabric

Supplies

Fabric scissors

Fusible seam tape

Measuring tape

Instructions

1. Determine desired length of drapes. Add 4½" to form rod pocket and allowance for hem.

2. Press ½" hem at top of panel. Turn again and press 3" hem, creating rod pocket. Apply fusible seam tape, following manufacturer's instructions and fuse into place.

3. Press a double ½" hem into bottom of panel. Apply fusible seam tape and fuse into place.

4. Feed curtain rod through rod pocket.

Comfortably Stuffed

Materials

Fabric: 1⅓ yd.

Polyester stuffing

Supplies

Fabric scissors

Fusible seam tape

Measuring tape

Instructions

1. Cut two 24" squares.

2. With right sides together, apply fusible seam tape along three sides and slightly around fourth corner, following manufacturer's instructions. Fuse together.

3. Clip each corner and turn right side out. Press corners and edges.

4. Stuff pillow loosely with polyester stuffing.

5. Apply fusible seam tape to opening and carefully fuse into place.

SUNDAY BRUNCH

MATERIALS

Fabric

Lace appliqués (8)

SUPPLIES

Fabric glue

Fabric marker

Fabric scissors

Ironing board and iron

Measuring tape

Lace appliqués can be made from vintage fabrics, doilies, thrift store wedding gowns, or formals. (I used the corners from placemats for this tablecloth and table runner.) Do not worry about leaving a raw edge on the appliqués. As the appliqués are adhered to the fabric, the fabric glue will prevent them from raveling.

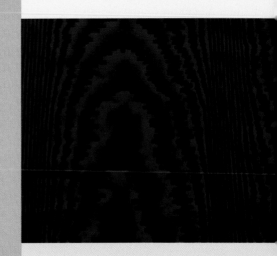

INSTRUCTIONS

1. Measure width and height of table. Cut fabric to these dimensions, allowing for drape.

2. Cut 18" x 72" piece of fabric for runner.

3. With wrong sides up, press and adhere ½" hem on all edges of both fabrics.

4. Place lace appliqués in each corner of both fabrics. Trace around appliqués. Adhere appliqués ¼" inside marked fabric. Cut away any fabric visible beneath appliqués.

FORMAL DINING

One type of trim was adhered around entire edge of table runner. A total of 6½ yards is needed. Various coordinating trims were adhered to each fused fabric piece, hiding fabric edges and creating a finished look.

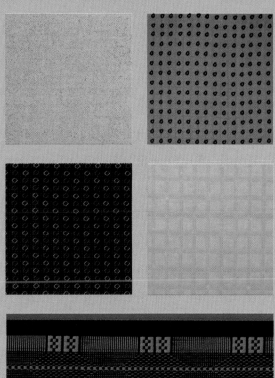

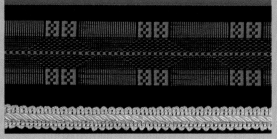

MATERIALS

Background fabrics, 54"-wide: ½ yd.; ½ yd.

Coordinating trims: 6 yds.

Trim: 6½ yds.

Two floral fabrics: ⅓ yd.; 1⅓ yd.

Tassels (2)

SUPPLIES

Fabric glue

Fabric marker

Fabric scissors

Fusible webbing

Measuring tape

INSTRUCTIONS

(Photo on page 124.)

1. Cut one 12" square and two 18½" x 46" pieces from first floral fabric. Cut two 12" squares from remaining floral fabric.

2. Cut two 13" x 5" pieces and two 18" squares from first background fabric. Cut two 3" x 48" pieces and two 3" x 18½" pieces from remaining background fabric.

3. Determine top and bottom of two 18" squares. Measure 8" up from bottom and mark. Draw a line from top center down diagonally to side markings. See Diagram A. Cut along dotted lines.

4. Apply fusible webbing to one end of each 18½" x 46" piece, following manufacturer's instructions. Fuse ends together, slightly overlapping, creating 18½" x 89" piece.

5. Place long fabric piece with wrong side up. Apply fusible webbing to entire piece. Place fabric pieces cut in Step 3 right side up onto each end of piece. See Diagram B.

6. Place remaining fabric pieces right side up onto fusible webbing as shown in Diagram C. Fuse all fabric pieces into place. Trim fabric on bottom to match fused pieces.

7. Cut trim as desired to fit around fused fabric pieces. Place tassel hanger through trim at runner end. See Diagram D. Adhere all trim.

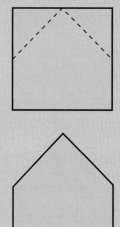

Diagram A

Diagram B

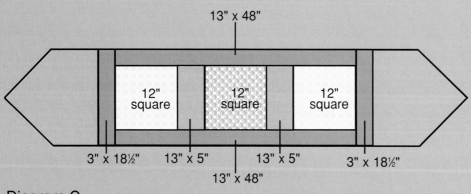

13" x 48"

12" square   12" square   12" square

3" x 18½"   13" x 5"   13" x 5"   3" x 18½"

13" x 48"

Diagram C

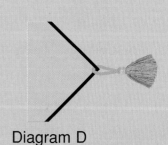

Diagram D

METRIC CONVERSION CHART

mm-millimetres cm-centimetres
inches to millimetres and centimetres

inches	mm	cm	inches	cm	inches	cm
⅛	3	0.3	9	22.9	30	76.2
¼	6	0.6	10	25.4	31	78.7
⅜	10	1.0	11	27.9	32	81.3
½	13	1.3	12	30.5	33	83.8
⅝	16	1.6	13	33.0	34	86.4
¾	19	1.9	14	35.6	35	88.9
⅞	22	2.2	15	38.1	36	91.4
1	25	2.5	16	40.6	37	94.0
1¼	32	3.2	17	43.2	38	96.5
1½	38	3.8	18	45.7	39	99.1
1¾	44	4.4	19	48.3	40	101.6
2	51	5.1	20	50.8	41	104.1
2½	64	6.4	21	53.3	42	106.7
3	76	7.6	22	55.9	43	109.2
3½	89	8.9	23	58.4	44	111.8
4	102	10.2	24	61.0	45	114.3
4½	114	11.4	25	63.5	46	116.8
5	127	12.7	26	66.0	47	119.4
6	152	15.2	27	68.6	48	121.9
7	178	17.8	28	71.1	49	124.5
8	203	20.3	29	73.7	50	127.0

yards to metres

yards	metres	yards	metres	yards	metres	yards	metres	yards	metres
⅛	0.11	2⅛	1.94	4⅛	3.77	6⅛	5.60	8⅛	7.43
¼	0.23	2¼	2.06	4¼	3.89	6¼	5.72	8¼	7.54
⅜	0.34	2⅜	2.17	4⅜	4.00	6⅜	5.83	8⅜	7.66
½	0.46	2½	2.29	4½	4.11	6½	5.94	8½	7.77
⅝	0.57	2⅝	2.40	4⅝	4.23	6⅝	6.06	8⅝	7.89
¾	0.69	2¾	2.51	4¾	4.34	6¾	6.17	8¾	8.00
⅞	0.80	2⅞	2.63	4⅞	4.46	6⅞	6.29	8⅞	8.12
1	0.91	3	2.74	5	4.57	7	6.40	9	8.23
1⅛	1.03	3⅛	2.86	5⅛	4.69	7⅛	6.52	9⅛	8.34
1¼	1.14	3¼	2.97	5¼	4.80	7¼	6.63	9¼	8.46
1⅜	1.26	3⅜	3.09	5⅜	4.91	7⅜	6.74	9⅜	8.57
1½	1.37	3½	3.20	5½	5.03	7½	6.86	9½	8.69
1⅝	1.49	3⅝	3.31	5⅝	5.14	7⅝	6.97	9⅝	8.80
1¾	1.60	3¾	3.43	5¾	5.26	7¾	7.09	9¾	8.92
1⅞	1.71	3⅞	3.54	5⅞	5.37	7⅞	7.20	9⅞	9.03
2	1.83	4	3.66	6	5.49	8	7.32	10	9.14

INDEX